I0479344

Table of Contents

Title

Conclusion

150+ Dropshipping Business Ideas

The online global has limitless business thoughts like dropshipping, where you could start your undertaking on-line without needing garage, delivery, or inventory. This phase explores greater than a hundred and fifty high-quality dropshipping business ideas for 2023, spanning numerous markets and niches. Whether you recall dropshipping a full-time profits circulate or a facet hustle, those thoughts will assist you be successful inside the international of dropshipping

150 Dropshipping Business Ideas The Easiest Way to Sell Online

By

Zula Russo

Chapter 01. Arts

Arts

The art market changed into one of the pleasant dropshipping business ideas 2021, as the enterprise had a 7.3% annual boom price that 12 months. With the developing price of the niche, it remains the exceptional option to invest in 2023. You can dropship some of the broadcast paintings and promote it online to make lots of greenbacks for each piece. Below are the maximum profitable and pleasant commercial enterprise ideas dropshipping within the artwork market:

Prints
- Children's art kits
- Greeting cards
- Phone cases
- Enamel pins
- Coloring books
- Wall Decor
- Art pencils
- 3D statues

Chapter 02. Books

Reading is progressively becoming the maximum famous pastime globally. Surveys display that approximately -thirds of america population study a print e-book ultimate 12 months. Despite the booming industry, selecting or that specialize in books with better demand and correct returns could be critical. The best options or categories of books to dropship encompass

Books Cetagory

Pre-K books
- Fiction
- Language books
- Non-fiction
- Large-print books
- Autobiographies
- Religious books

Chapter 03. Jewelry

Jewelry is one of the growing dropshipping business ideas in India and global. Market records show consumers spend about $28.68 billion yearly on jewelry merchandise. With the massive capability, you can make money on line by means of dropshipping and promoting those products at a profit. Necklaces, block gold jewelry, and earrings are steadily getting returned into the jewelry. Below are the most worthwhile merchandise you may remember for dropshipping:

Gold hoop earrings
- Necklaces
- Block gold rings
- Bracelets
- Gemstones
- Wedding rings
- Anniversary jewelry
- Costume jewelry
- Fine Jewelry

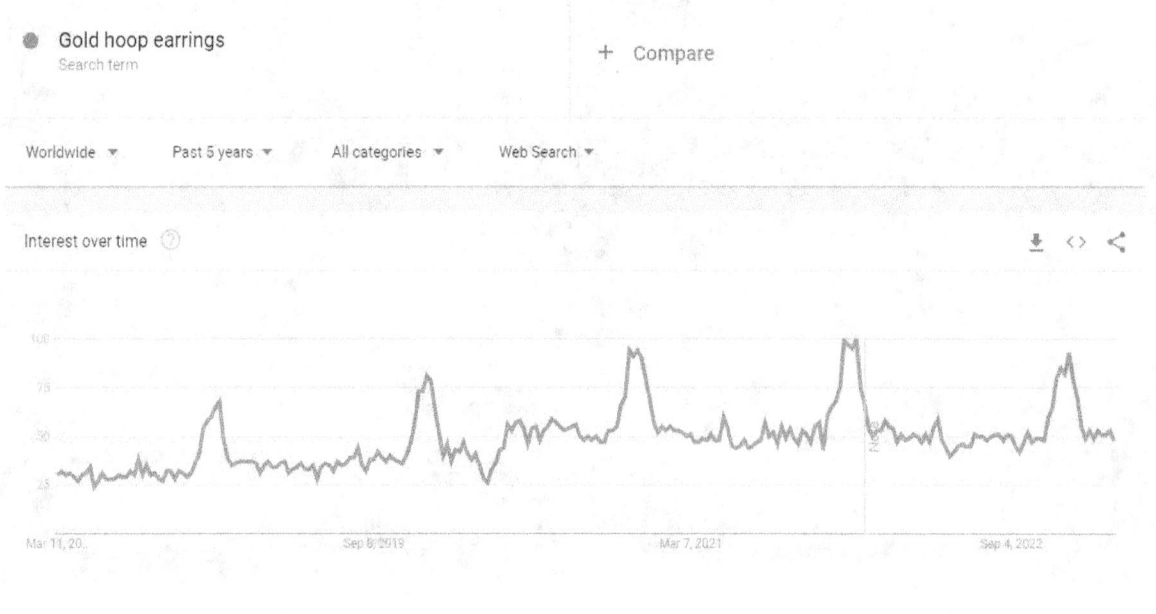

Chapter 04. Beauty and skincare

Statistics show an ever-increasing trend in call for for non-public care and beauty products. With specialists defensive the industry to be worth $679.79 billion in 2025, you could declare your stake within the enterprise. Many people spend on products that clear up diverse cosmetic-related fitness problems and look. You can supply those products from authentic sellers and promote them at a income. The popular business name ideas for dropshipping on this zone encompass:

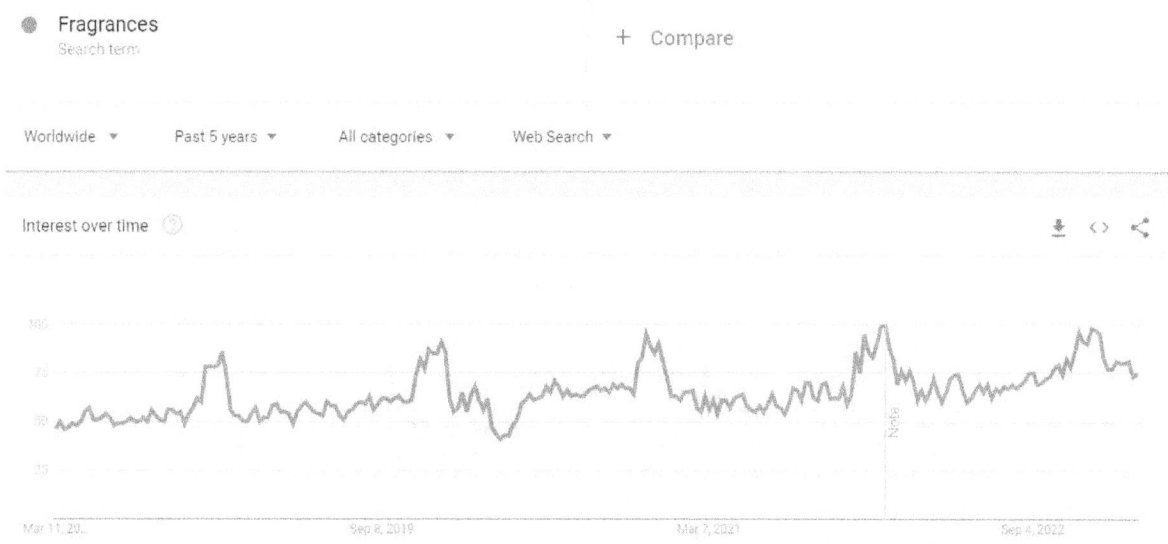

Lip balm
- Cleansers
- Moisturizer
- Concealer
- Foundation
- Fragrances
- Makeup bags and brushes
- Nail clippers
- Cooling eye masks
- Sunscreen
- Acne treatment
- Facial rollers
- Hair straighteners
- Beard trimmers

Chapter 05. Coffee

Studies display that most Americans drink about cups of coffee each day. The non-stop call for and uptake for coffee have grown the industry, with professionals tipping its fee at $a hundred and fifty five billion via 2026. Finding a good espresso dropshipping dealer is a fantastic way to take your slice or get a great income from this area of interest. Here are the top and maximum worthwhile items you could dropship inside the espresso industry:

Flavored syrups
- Coffee grinders
- Coffee bags
- Coffee pods
- Sachets
- Coffee beans

Chapter 06. Clothing and accessories

The range of people attempting to find garb and athleisure has elevated for the reason that pandemic. Experts see the worldwide clothing enterprise as the biggest on-line market in the world, with a valuation of $1.Five trillion. The clothing and add-ons comprise the fashion niche and different garb. Studies have shown the growing popularity of sports bras, leggings, and other garb in preceding years. Therefore, you can begin dropshipping these products and begin being profitable online. The dropshipping commercial enterprise names thoughts on this class include

Sports bras
- Hoodies
- Socks
- Hats
- T-shirts
- Fancy dress costumes
- Fashion accessories
- Bridesmaid dresses
- Cargo pants
- Swimming trunks

Chapter 08. Fitness products

With the spread of covid-19 forcing maximum people to work from home, there was an accelerated want for exercise. Most individuals had to put money into fitness products and tools to workout. Thus, health merchandise became one of the most worthwhile dropshipping enterprise thoughts 2022. Since then, health merchandise, such as health trackers, have emerge as popular searches at the internet. Besides the fitness trackers, there are other workout merchandise you may take into account dropping shop this 12 months. These merchandise and device consist of

Fitness trackers
- Resistance bands
- Step blocks
- Trampolines
- Fitness trackers
- Protein powders
- Jump ropes
- Gym gloves
- Foam rollers
- Yoga mats

Chapter 09. Baby products

Caregivers and mother and father spend about $sixty seven.35 billion annually purchasing diverse infant care products. With the growing demand for this product, professionals task the industry to hit $88.Seventy two billion in 2026. We've were given numerous area of interest markets you could discover in the baby space or industry. For instance, since 2016, there has been an growth inside the range of searches for gender monitor balloons to help soon-to-be mother and father get the infant's gender. Below are some baby products you could do not forget to beautify your dropshipping business idea:

- Gender reveal balloons
- Kids' toys ● Diapers
- Strollers ● Baby carriers
- Stair gates
- Organic baby foods
- Breast milk pumps
- Booster seats
- Baby carriers
- Changing mats
- Baby monitors

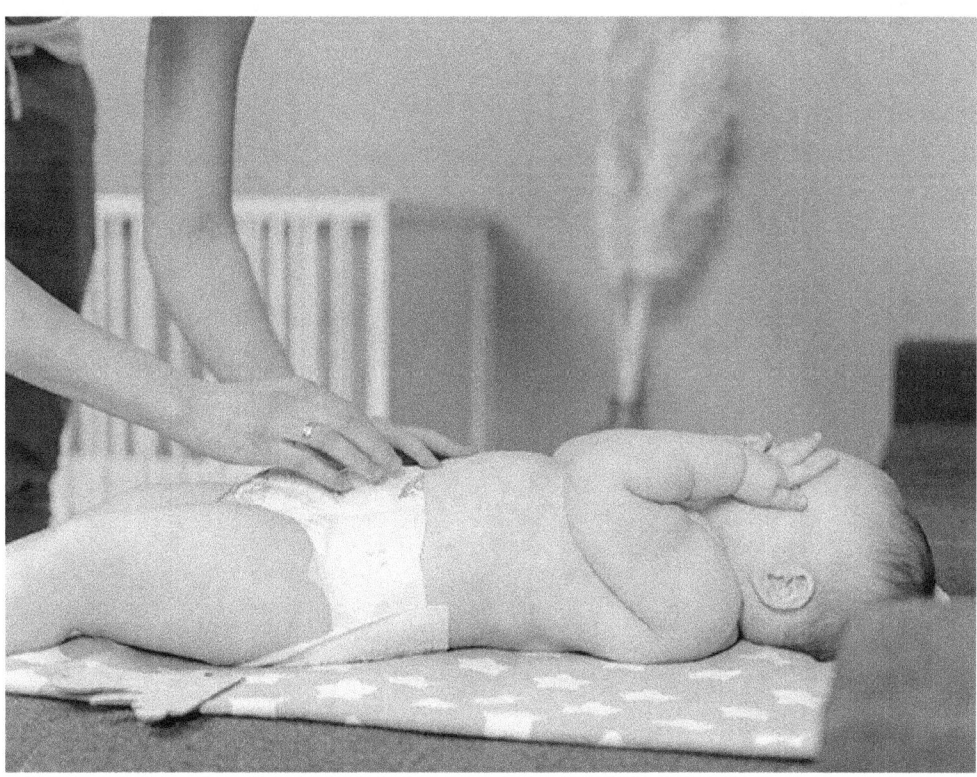

Chapter 10. CBD products

Over the past two years, statistics show that more than 64 million Americans have used CBD products. These products contain various hemp-derived ingredients that offer a wide range of health and overall well-being benefits. You can start dropshipping various CBD products and selling them online to your customers. Nevertheless, it'll be good to understand your state's laws and regulations on dropshipping CBD products. The best dropshipping business name ideas in this niche include:

CBD sprays
- Bath bombs
- Pet CBD oils
- Lotions and Creams
- CBD tinctures
- Supplements
- CBD oils

Chapter 11. Electronics and digital appliances

The global expenditure on electronics, which include cameras, computer systems, and so on., is about $376 billion every year. You make cash with the aid of checking the product in short supply and in greater demand for dropshipping on numerous platforms. Nevertheless, with the niche having severa guidelines, make sure which you check the goods rigorously to make sure they meet the proper protection requirements. The maximum trending dropshipping business name ideas on this enterprise encompass the following:

Chargers
- Cameras
- Headphones
- Printer ink
- Sat navs
- Screen cleaners
- Smart speakers
- Phone cases
- TV remote controls
- Kettles
- Flash disks
- Smart speakers
- Memory cards

Chapter 12. Home tools

Experts predict that the house improvement income market can hit 621.3 billion by 2025. The mission makes this niche one of the most important and maximum profitable client markets. The area of interest encompasses numerous products from hardware, redecorating accessories, and domestic devices to help you construct a worthwhile enterprise. With the growing need for those products, you could make a number of money by means of dropshipping extraordinary home equipment. Here are the pinnacle home-associated gadgets you can bear in mind for dropshipping:

Doorbells
- Extension leads
- Step ladders
- Security cameras
- Wine fridges
- Lint removers
- Modern lights
- Decoration equipment
- Carpet cleaners
- Handheld vacuums

Chapter 13. Furniture

From home furniture to offices or places of work, there has been a surge in call for for fixtures. The growing demand makes this area of interest one of the most profitable dropshipping enterprise call ideas. Besides the accelerated call for, you can make massive income as most dealers typically sell small home improvement devices at a higher rate. Thus, with the assets dropshipping and marketing approach, you could make a kill with this project. For example, tremendous product images to build patron accept as true with and resolve the patron's pre-buy anxiety. Here are the worthwhile furniture-associated products to dropship

Lamps
● Rugs
● Bookshelves
● Bean bags
● Mirrors
● Standing desks
● Home office chairs
● Shelving units
● Dining chairs

Chapter 14. Pet products

With the range of American families proudly owning a puppy increasing, the price of the industry has skyrocketed to $123.6 billion. You maximize the income from this enterprise through finding the quality dropshipping business idea within the area of interest. For example, canine vitamins are one of the excellent dropshipping business ideas you may keep in mind in the pet merchandise enterprise. Most proprietors spend chunks of cash to purchase these dietary supplements to decorate their canine's health. Here are some merchandise you can maximize in this industry:

Dog supplements, including vitamins
- Pet food
- Pet leashes
- Cat litter
- Collars
- Bird seeds
- Raw bones
- Grass patches
- Slow-feeding bowls
- Pet ID tags
- Drying coats
- Cage water bottles
- Pet beddings
- Toys
- Grooming supplies

Chapter 15. Car Accessories

Studies show that the automobile industry sells approximately 65 million motors every 12 months. With the growing quantity of automobile proprietors, you could make money on-line by way of dropshipping vehicle components and accessories to them. You can remember Tik Tok as an concept for the nice dropshipping ideas in this area of interest. In addition, you operate insights from Amazon whilst sourcing car add-ons to your dropshipping venture. The popular and maximum worthwhile alternatives include:

Car mats
- Air fresheners
- Cup holders
- Car cleaning kits
- Wiper blades
- Trunk organizers
- Tablet holders
- Neck pillows
- Car hoovers
- Steering wheel covers

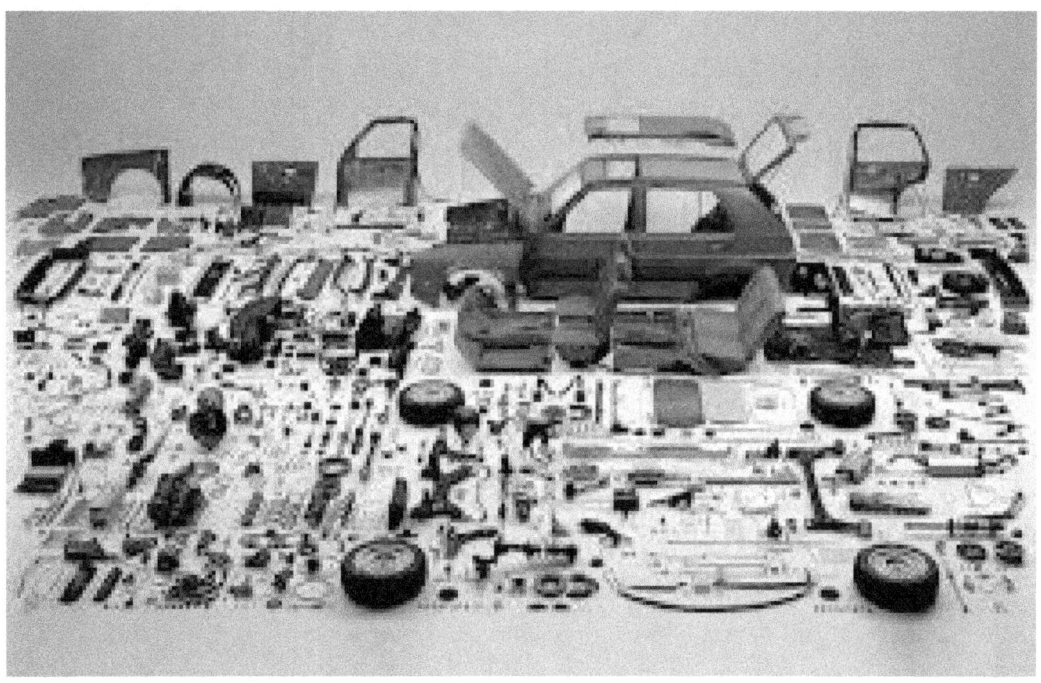

Chapter 16. Outdoor gear and apparel

Outdoor equipment and clothing were one of the top dropshipping commercial enterprise thoughts 2022. Statistics show that the market had grown to about $34.Eight billion in that year. With the expert projecting a similarly boom of about $45 billion that year, it's one of the most respectable and worthwhile dropshipping thoughts you can venture into this year. The outside gear and apparel niche is a wide enterprise with numerous options you can recollect for dropshipping. Here are the most famous and worthwhile options:

Backpacks
- Camping or hiking tents
- Fishing rods
- Binoculars
- Hiking apparel footwear
- Sleeping bags
- Outdoor accessories
- Climbing equipment

Chapter 17. Eco-friendly products

With anybody working toward the use of environmentally pleasant and sustainable merchandise, this industry is growing into one of the maximum worthwhile ventures. Research suggests that purchasers globally are inclined to pay extra for eco-friendly and sustainable merchandise. With most customers opting to pay extra for those products, you can maximize the income by dropshipping exceptional famous eco-friendly products to the customers. You can bear in mind the subsequent profitable green products:

Cloth shopping bags
- Bamboo utensils
- Reusable water bottles

Chapter 18. Sportswear

Besides fitness tools, sports wear is likewise another dropshipping idea you may use to make earnings on line. The sports activities gear stages from certified sports products to exercising gadget and athletic apparel. Experts discovered that the marketplace for retail sports clothing inside the United States turned into kind of fifty three billion in 2020. Since then, there has been a surge within the demand for sports clothing profits, making it one of the maximum worthwhile ventures. You could make cash on-line through dropshipping the following in-demand sports activities garb and shoes:

Sport boots
- Timers
- Water Bottles
- Knee braces
- Posture corrector
- Balance boards
- Compression socks
- Kinesiology tape
- Running pouches
- Sports sunglasses

Chapter 19. Healthcare and wellness products

The adverse results of covid-19 and the containment measures to control the ailment changed global health shipping. Most people opted for digital health, which includes using on line products to beautify good fitness and wellbeing. With the growing demand for these merchandise, you could pick numerous precise merchandise for dropshipping. Nevertheless, you'll need clinical heritage or know-how to achieve this area of interest. Below are the pinnacle dropshipping commercial enterprise thoughts you can do not forget inside the healthcare products enterprise:

Sleep Mask
- Sweat Belt
- Anti Snoring Device
- Posture Corrector Brace
- Anti Smoking Magnetic Patch
- Ultrasound Cavitation Device
- Neck Massager
- Electric Muscular Stimulator
- Hair Growth Serum

Chapter 20. Sex toys

Sex remains one of the maximum pleasing sports between partners or couples. With the need for satisfaction, many individuals have invested in diverse merchandise to strive new matters and decorate their sexual revel in. Statistics predict that the e-trade intercourse toy market will develop from $12.Three billion in 2020 to $18.1 billion through 2026. With the anticipated boom, you may sell and make a income online by dropshipping trending intercourse toys and other accessories. Here are the maximum famous alternatives you can remember:

Wand & clitoral vibrators
- Dildos ● Butt plugs
- Sex dolls ● Cock rings
- Lingerie
- Fetishwear for both men and women;
- Massage oils
- Water-based lubes

Above are the pinnacle dropshipping enterprise thoughts you may select for 2023. Nevertheless, when deciding on a selected product or niche, make sure you keep in mind the traits, demand, profit margin, and opposition to choose the maximum profitable ones.

Chapter 21. How to Find a Dropshipping Idea

Finding the proper and profitable commercial enterprise idea dropshipping is important for beginning a a hit on line commercial enterprise. With the severa options, it may be tough to get a profitable and particular area of interest. Here is the right manual on a way to find dropshipping thoughts.

TikTok
- Marketplace bestsellers
- Pinterest trends
- TredHunter
- Niche-specific forums and blogs

Tik Tok

TikTok is one of the top social media structures that you may use to get the exceptional dropshipping concept. Approximately fifty five% of customers have bought a product after seeing it on Tik Tok. Scan thru the #TikTokMadeMeBuyIt hashtag to find out your next worthwhile dropshipping concept. You also can get the maximum trending or on-demand product via engaging with the patron on your related industry. After getting the concept, get similar merchandise from official providers and promote them at a profit. Experts suggest specializing in content material or products associated with your selected area of interest or industry.

Marketplace bestsellers

With the developing recognition of market bestsellers, experts are expecting that with the aid of 2027, they'll be key in about 59% of the trading journey. Thus, you can don't forget them the satisfactory choice to discover profitable and trending dropshipping commercial enterprise call thoughts. You can begin this strategy by means of checking the pinnacle product' pages on Walmart, Etsy, and Amazon. Besides these pages, you may also find the first-class thoughts by searching on wholesale marketplaces like Alibaba, SaleHoo, and

Globalsources. GlobalSources facilitates consumers get the suitable alternative by using supplying the great dropshipping thoughts.

Pinterest trends

Pinterest is a popular seek engine and social media hybrid that permits users to shop extraordinary pins on a digital motherboard. How can you operate Pinterest to get the fine dropshipping thoughts in India? You can use this platform to test what the opposite customers have stored all through the week or month. For instance, you may use it to discover trending and famous pins in the ultimate week or month. You can dropship comparable products in your online store with this records.

TredHunter

This platform uses synthetic intelligence, research teams, and web page view records to find out the top and trending merchandise. For instance, current examples of trending products include muted purple shoes and compostable menswear. Despite those products trending during the last few weeks or months, you can use the platform to search for your unique products. You can search or browse the internet site to test pinnacle on line investment ideas before the marketplace saturates. With the records, you could decide on the high-quality and maximum worthwhile merchandise to invest in.

Niche-specific forums and blogs

Did you know that you can discover a dropshipping idea by means of checking area of interest-particular blogs and forums? You can use boards and blogs associated with your niche or enterprise to get insights into the worthwhile products in call for. Search for the top and applicable forums or blogs to test what other people are discussing. The dialogue will help you have got an concept of a worthwhile venture or business call ideas for dropshipping. You also can start discussions or ask questions to help you get remarks on profitable product ideas. Besides getting the most profitable dropshipping concept, you may additionally use these blogs to recognize what's nice for your target market.

Chapter 22. How to Choose a Dropshipping Business Idea

While dropshipping is one of the low-risk commercial enterprise fashions, it's crucial to validate the thoughts before you challenge into it. Choosing a worthwhile dropshipping enterprise concept enables construct a a hit on line funding. Here are the pinnacle suggestions that will help you pick a worthwhile dropshipping business idea:

Consider seasonality and trends
- Evaluate the demand
- Check your competition
- Find a reputable dropshipping supplier
- Order a sample
- Survey your target market
- Calculate the profit margin
- Consider the marketing and branding strategy

Consider seasonality and trends

When looking for a dropshipping enterprise concept, it's very important to don't forget seasonality and traits. Why is it important to take into account these factors? These elements make certain that you select profitable and trending products with long-term potential. Tools like Social media insights and Google Trends also can help you discover trending and seasonal products.

Evaluate the demand

Evaluating the call for is fundamental before running or beginning your subsequent dropshipping concept. It helps you test whether individuals or your target audience are talking about the products you need to start promoting. You can use equipment like Google traits for studies. Google Trends provides historic statistics on the number of individuals who've looked for particular dropshipping business ideas. It'll be smart to take note of keywords with an upward trend, because it indicates they're famous and feature increased demand.

Check your competition

Experts endorse which you take a look at the opposition in your chosen niche. With enterprise thoughts like dropshipping requiring a a success advertising and marketing method, you'll should pay greater for paid ads. In addition, there can be more competition for key phrases for top products. Thus, building a profitable enterprise is essential to taking part in the nice returns.

The ideal opposition level will rely upon the business kind you want to build. For example, low competition is good when struggling to discover outlets with comparable merchandise. In assessment, with excessive opposition, you have to do not forget the excellent pricing method as there's demand for the goods.

Find reputable dropshipping suppliers

These providers can both wreck or make your new enterprise assignment. Dropshipping suppliers are chargeable for manufacturing, creating, packing, and turning in the orders. Ensure that the dropshipping business concept you pick out has professional suppliers. While you can recollect providers like Alibaba, Aliexpress, and Wholesale2B, GlobalSources continue to be the exceptional and most dependable wholesale dealer you can believe.

Order a sample

While dropshipping is a commercial enterprise which you don't have money to begin, your potential purchaser will best pay for awesome products. When choosing the great dropshipping concept, request a sample to test if it is really worth paying that quantity. Experts endorse that it has a decrease fee fee and superb whilst you're searching out the best dropshipping idea to make you the maximum income.

Survey your target market

The goal market includes the folks who'll be purchasing your products. It'll be essential to survey your goal market and audience to check the call for, the satisfactory advertising and marketing channel, and the amount they're inclined to pay for the product. Ensure you get insights into those that will help you select the most worthwhile and in-call for products to fit your targeted audience.

Calculate the profit margin

The first-class dropshipping thoughts are with merchandise you may source at a decrease price and resell at better charges to generate earnings. Thus, it'll be vital to calculate the profit margin earlier than finding out to project into the enterprise. You can use the loose earnings margin calculator to check the quantity you'll stay with purchasing the product and buying the choosing, packing, and transport expenses. Experts propose you cross for cheaper products and sell at a excessive fee or consciousness on awesome clients to boom your earnings margin.

Consider the branding and marketing strategies

Your desired advertising and marketing and branding strategies will let you in deciding on the fine dropshipping thoughts. Your selected business idea need to resonate with your preferred advertising method and target market. For instance, if you plan on the usage of social media advertising, make certain the goods you pick out to resonate with the target market. It's an vital tip that helps you choose the excellent and most worthwhile dropshipping commercial enterprise names enterprise.

Conclusion

Dropshipping may be the most rewarding and rewarding manner to begin an internet enterprise project. While it's a moneymaking way to start an internet task, selecting the proper dropshipping ideas can be key to your achievement. The numerous dropshipping niche and products make it difficult to choose the most successful and profitable one.

Conducting a market, opposition, call for, studies, and calculating the profit margin allow you to discover the great and most worthwhile dropshipping thoughts. Fashion, beauty & health, electronics, puppy foods, sportswear, out of doors equipment, CBD products, jewelry, and car add-ons are a number of the satisfactory options.

After selecting the most profitable dropshipping business concept, getting a reliable source for wholesale merchandise will enhance your achievement. GlobalSources.Com is a dependable and official source for getting wholesale products. The platform gives diverse extremely good products at competitive charges and connects you with trusted providers international.